World of Mammals

# Dolphins

by Connie Colwell Miller

**Consultant:**
Jaime R. Alvarado Bremer, PhD
Departments of Marine Biology and Wildlife and Fisheries Sciences
Texas A&M University
Galveston, Texas

Capstone
press

Mankato, Minnesota

Bridgestone Books are published by Capstone Press,
151 Good Counsel Drive, P.O. Box 669, Mankato, Minnesota 56002.
www.capstonepress.com

*Library of Congress Cataloging-in-Publication Data*
Miller, Connie Colwell, 1976–
    Dolphins / by Connie Colwell Miller.
        p. cm.—(Bridgestone Books. World of mammals.)
    Summary: "A brief introduction to dolphins, discussing their characteristics, habitat, life cycle, and
predators. Includes a range map, life cycle illustration, and amazing facts"—Provided by publisher.
    Includes bibliographical references and index.
    ISBN 0-7368-4310-8 (hardcover)
    1. Dolphins—Juvenile literature. I. Title. II. Series: Bridgestone Books. World of mammals.
QL737.C432M54 2006
599.53—dc22                                         2004028431

**Editorial Credits**

Shari Joffe, editor; Molly Nei, set designer; Biner Design, book designer; Patricia Rasch, illustrator;
    Kelly Garvin, photo researcher; Scott Thoms, photo editor

**Photo Credits**

Ardea London Ltd./Francois Gohier, 6
Corel, 1
Jeff Rotman, 16
Seapics.com/Doug Perrine, 12, 18, 20; Ingrid Visser, cover
Tom & Pat Leeson, 4
Tom Stack & Associates, Inc./Wildlife Images/Michael S. Nolan, 10

1 2 3 4 5 6 10 09 08 07 06 05

# Table of Contents

# Dolphins

A dolphin soars out of the waves. It looks around, then dives back into the ocean. Dolphins often breach, or jump out of the water.

Dolphins are sea **mammals**. Like land mammals, dolphins have backbones and are **warm-blooded**. They also breathe air through lungs and must come to the surface often.

Dolphins are part of a group of mammals called toothed whales. Thirty-two types of dolphins live in the world's oceans. Killer whales and pilot whales are considered dolphins.

◀ A bottlenose dolphin breaches.

# What Dolphins Look Like

Dolphins have long, smooth bodies. Bottlenose dolphins are gray. Atlantic spotted dolphins are gray with spots. Killer whales are black and white.

A dolphin has two flippers, a **dorsal fin** on its back, and a flat tail. Dolphins swim by moving their tails up and down. The two **flukes** on a dolphin's tail help the dolphin turn and stop. The flippers and dorsal fin help the dolphin steer through the water.

◀ A dolphin uses its powerful tail to speed through the water.

# Dolphin Range Map

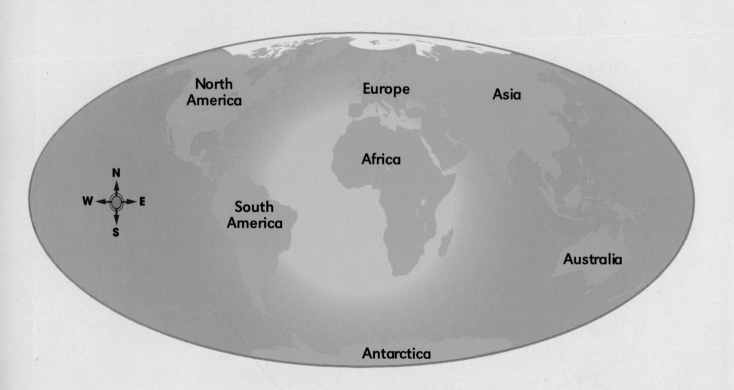

Where Dolphins Live

# Dolphins in the World

Dolphins swim in every ocean and sea of the world. Most kinds of dolphins live in warm waters near the equator. Others live in colder waters to the north or south. Killer whales and bottlenose dolphins live in both warm and cold waters of the world.

# Dolphin Habitats

Dolphins live in saltwater **habitats**. Salt water keeps a dolphin's skin soft and wet. Dolphins may live close to the shore or in deeper waters. They spend most of their time underwater. They come up to the surface when they need air.

Some dolphins travel in large groups called pods. Common dolphins can travel in pods with thousands of members. Other dolphins travel in smaller groups.

◀ Killer whales swim in both coastal waters (left) and open seas.

# What Dolphins Eat

Dolphins eat fish, squid, and shrimp. They do not chew their food. Dolphins use sharp teeth to grab their food. They then swallow the food whole.

Dolphins sometimes work together to catch fish. A pod of dolphins surrounds a school of fish. They swim in circles to keep the fish from escaping. The dolphins then take turns eating the fish.

◀ Long-beaked common dolphins chase a school of sardines.

# The Life Cycle of a Dolphin

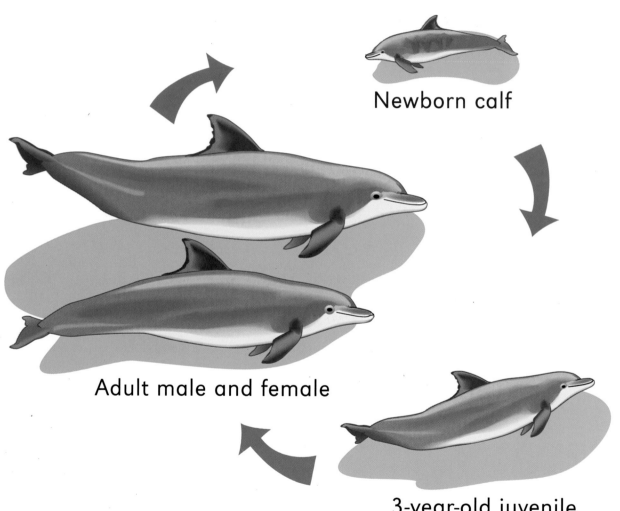

Newborn calf

Adult male and female

3-year-old juvenile

# Producing Young

Male and female dolphins **mate** in the spring or summer. Males make popping sounds to make females come near. The dolphins often rub noses before mating.

A female gives birth to a calf about 12 months later. Other female dolphins help the mother give birth. The calf is born just under the surface of the water. The mother gently pushes the calf to the surface for its first breath of air.

# Growing Up

A dolphin calf drinks milk from its mother for about 18 months. Calves begin eating fish when they are about three or four months old. Their teeth begin to form at that age.

The dolphins in a pod watch over each other's calves. One female may take care of several calves while other mothers hunt for food. A dolphin calf stays near its mother for three to six years.

◄ A dolphin calf swims next to its mother.

# Dangers to Dolphins

Dolphins have a few **predators**. Sharks and killer whales sometimes attack calves. To protect their calves, adults may ram predators with their noses.

People are the greatest danger to dolphins. Tuna fishers catch dolphins in their nets by accident. Dolphins get tangled in the nets and drown. People sometimes pollute the waters where dolphins live.

Researchers study dolphins to find ways to protect them. Many groups are working to protect dolphins in the future.

◀ Researchers work closely with dolphins to learn as much as they can about them.

# Amazing Facts about Dolphins

- A dolphin breathes through a blowhole on top of its head.
- Dolphins sleep near the surface of the water. They rest only half of their brain at a time. The other half stays awake so that the dolphin remembers to rise to the surface and breathe.
- Dolphins are very smart. They learn quickly and can solve hard problems.
- Bottlenose dolphins can jump as high as 16 feet (4.9 meters) in the air.

◀ A dolphin takes a breath through its blowhole.

# Glossary

**dorsal fin** (DOR-suhl FIN)—the fin located on an animal's back

**fluke** (FLOOK)—the wide, flat area at the end of a dolphin's tail

**habitat** (HAB-uh-tat)—the place and natural conditions where an animal lives

**mammal** (MAM-uhl)—a warm-blooded animal that has a backbone; female mammals feed milk to their young.

**mate** (MAYT)—to join together to produce young

**predator** (PRED-uh-tur)—an animal that hunts other animals for food

**warm-blooded** (warm-BLUHD-id)—having a body temperature that stays the same

# Read More

**Laskey, Elizabeth.** *Dolphins.* Sea Creatures. Chicago: Heinemann Library, 2003.

**Richardson, Adele D.** *Dolphins: Fins, Flippers, and Flukes.* The Wild World of Animals. Mankato, Minn.: Bridgestone Books, 2001.

# Internet Sites

FactHound offers a safe, fun way to find Internet sites related to this book. All of the sites on FactHound have been researched by our staff.

Here's how:
1. Visit *www.facthound.com*
2. Type in this special code **0736843108** for age-appropriate sites. Or enter a search word related to this book for a more general search.
3. Click on the **Fetch It** button.

FactHound will fetch the best sites for you!

# Index